CW01072256

YOUR FUTURE BY
READING THE CARDS

AN INTRODUCTION TO CARTOMANCY

YOUR FUTURE BY READING THE CARDS

FRANCIS A. BEVAN

ANGUS
& ROBERTSON
PUBLISHERS

ANGUS & ROBERTSON PUBLISHERS

Unit 4, Eden Park, 31 Waterloo Road,
North Ryde, NSW, Australia 2113, and
16 Golden Square, London W1R 4BN,
United Kingdom

This book is copyright.
Apart from any fair dealing for the
purposes of private study, research,
criticism or review, as permitted
under the Copyright Act, no part may
be reproduced by any process without
written permission. Inquiries should
be addressed to the publishers.

First published in Australia
by Angus & Robertson Publishers in 1986
First published in the United Kingdom
by Angus & Robertson in 1986

Copyright © Francis A. Bevan

National Library of Australia
Cataloguing-in-publication data.

Bevan, Francis A. (Francis Alexander), 1962-
    Your future by reading the cards.

    ISBN 0 207 15321 3.

    1. Fortune-telling by cards. I. Title.

133.3'242

Designed by April Briscoe

Typeset in 11/12pt Apollo

Printed in Australia
by the Dominion Press–Hedges & Bell

This book could not have been written without the support and love of my mother, Doreen Bevan, Noel and Denise, my closest and dearest friend Terry, and the presence of Grant MacDonaldson and Rosanna Vertom. It could not have been completed without the valuable contributions made by Verna, Andrew, Tony, Jeff and Karen.

CONTENTS

Part I   Meanings and Methods   3

INTRODUCTION 1

ANCESTRY OF THE CARDS 5

OLD WIVES' TALES
OF THE CARDS 7

TECHNIQUES OF CARTOMANCY 9

INTERPRETATIONS OF
EACH CARD 15

THE 36 CARD PACK 23

CARDS IN COMBINATION 29

INTERPRETATIONS OF
CARD GROUPS 33

PAST, PRESENT AND FUTURE 35

ASTROLOGY BY THE CARDS 39

DELLA'S METHOD 45

YOUR DESTINY IN 52 CARDS 49

THE ROMANY METHOD 53

QUESTIONS AND ANSWERS 57

Part II   Fortune-telling Games   61

POETIC FORTUNE-TELLING 63

YOUR WEEK BY THE CARDS 69

PERSONALITIES BY THE CARDS 77

YOUR PERFECT PARTNER 85

Part III   Case Histories   87

CARD READINGS 89
CONCLUSION 101
GLOSSARY 103

INTRODUCTION

Over the centuries, in many different cultures and in many different ways, soothsayers have attempted to predict the future. Ordinary playing cards are often used, their symbols being interpreted to relate to various events and types of people. Fortune-telling is, perhaps, a unique way to develop psychic powers and one of the easiest ways to do this is by learning to read the hidden meaning in playing cards. By doing this it may be possible to learn some of the things one needs to know to improve one's future.

The very words "fortune-telling" tend to instil a feeling of mysticism in people, especially when they first look into this ancient art. Almost automatically they ask questions such as "What does my future hold?" and "How can it be told?". These questions have been asked since the beginning of time and numerous ways have been devised to attempt to solve the riddle of looking into the future. Perhaps the most common method used has been the cards, although most clairvoyants would agree that this is only one way of predicting the future.

Unfortunately, most books on cartomancy, as the art of card-reading is known, tend to obscure rather than clarify it.

In this book, therefore, I have attempted to present the ancient art of fortune-telling by the cards in such a way that it can be easily used by beginners.

The basic meaning of each card and the way the cards should be laid out has been described in a simple and straightforward manner.

Although few people have the time to make a complete study of fortune-telling, there is much to be learned from even a basic introduction into this art, and I feel that the cards are by far the easiest and most simple way to begin.

The best way to become proficient at the art of cartomancy is by constant practice. After a while each card will seem to develop its own "personality", making the readings fairly easy and enjoyable.

INTRODUCTION

Your Future by Reading the Cards is arranged in three parts. Part I outlines the history of cards and card-reading, gives all the meanings of the cards (both for single cards and for combinations of cards), and describes the various methods of reading cards. These methods include using the cards to look at the past, present and future; combining astrology and cartomancy; using the normal 52 card pack or a 36 card pack; and various methods of card-reading devised by different people throughout history.

Part II describes card-reading games for parties. As well as enlivening many a social gathering, these games can provide players with valuable insights into themselves and their lives.

Part III provides a selection of case histories from the author's professional clairvoyant experience. These examples demonstrate how the cards have helped him to develop his psychic powers.

PART I
MEANINGS AND
METHODS

ANCESTRY OF THE CARDS

The ancient Egyptians were the first people to develop and design any type of card. The first known pack of cards is said to be the ancient Tarot pack, which was used for the purposes of divination and for other deep mystical reasons. However, a discussion on the deeper meaning of Tarot cards is beyond the scope of this book.

The ancient Tarot pack consists of two parts, called the major and minor arcanas. Today's playing cards are derived from the minor arcana, the only exception being the Joker, which coincides with the Fool of the major arcana. The Knight of the major arcana has been omitted from the court cards, leaving only the four Kings, Queens and Jacks.

The four suits of the minor arcana in the ancient Tarot pack represent the four seasons — summer, autumn, winter and spring; the four times of day — dawn, noon, afternoon and dusk; and the four ages of man — childhood, teenage, adulthood and old age. The four suits of the ordinary playing cards refer to certain events and conditions. Clubs relate to success, travel and alterations. Hearts relate to romance, one's desires or the emotions. Diamonds relate to money and financial situations, whereas the Spades relate to unpleasant happenings like sicknesses and tragedies. The court cards, however, normally indicate particular types of people.

Probably the first race of people known to use ordinary playing cards as a means of predicting the future were the Gipsies. This nomadic race is said to be descended from a low caste of Hindus who were driven from their homeland in India, found their way through western Asia into Egypt and from northern Africa into Europe. The Gipsies are renowned for all types of fortune-telling, from the cards to scattering straw. Through years of persecution they have deepened their intuition and used it to assert their powers over their oppressors.

These Romany folk have kept the ancient art of cartomancy from the East intact, while most people today use playing cards for amusement or for gambling.

For centuries, the design and the suits of playing cards varied enormously, and even the number of cards in a pack varied at different times and in different places between 36 and 78 cards. Among the examples of different suit symbols are Chinese cards, which used coins; Indian cards, in which suits were represented by animals; and Italian packs, which had swords, cups, coins and wands. The cards took on their present suits during the 1500s, although there are still some variations in different countries.

Like other forms of art, court-card design has reflected the taste of individual artists. The cards used in the English-speaking world today show the Jacks, Queens and Kings dressed in clothing of the reign of Britain's Henry VII (1457–85).

The backs of the cards have also undergone many changes. Early cards had plain backs, but by the nineteenth century back-design had become an important feature of card manufacture, in order to avoid suspicion of a "marked" deck.

The development of the design of the Jack of Clubs in English playing cards.

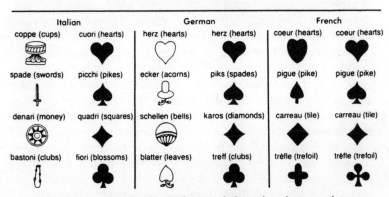

The ancient and modern forms of suit symbols used on playing cards in Italy, Germany and France.

OLD WIVES' TALES
OF THE CARDS

Since the beginning of time many strange stories have been associated with these simply decorated pieces of cardboard. As far back as the Middle Ages the practice of cartomancy was regarded as an evil cult and severe penalties were placed upon those who practised it. For this reason the names and symbols on the cards were changed. Several churches and government bodies all over Europe banned cartomancy, although gamblers continued to practise it.

Perhaps the card best known for its tale of woe is the Ace of Spades because of its association with evil. It was originally used as a stamp denoting that the playing card tax had been paid. Those who tried to evade the tax were severely punished and sometimes cruel penalties were imposed upon them. "The Plaie of Cardes is an invention of the Devill", wrote John Northbrooke in 1579 and other authors called them "The Devil's Picture Book". The Spanish omitted the Queen as it was considered unacceptable to include her in the Devil's Pack.

Several Protestant countries in northern Europe, namely Finland, Sweden and Denmark, regarded card playing as being associated with the devil, who was said to appear whenever the cards were dealt and to sit under the card table. During the game if anybody blasphemed the Devil was said to leap up and stand behind the blasphemer. The Devil was said to have taken many forms, one being a black cat, another a black dog with a card clutched in its paw.

Card games and cartomancy had become so popular, that in 1423 St Bernadino of Sienna preached an anti-gambling sermon and disapproval started to spread. Puritans deemed it a sin to keep a pack of cards in the house.

John Wesley saw to it that they were forbidden in the Constitution of the Methodist Church, and other churches followed, agreeing that games of chance, which offered something for nothing, could only be a source of temptation and sin. Cards were held in such awe that it was even considered bad luck to steal them. Fishermen and miners avoided carrying them at work because they were said to bring bad luck.

Church opposition to ordinary card games lessened when high stakes ceased to be the rule. However, this did not apply to the art of cartomancy.

There are still those even today who fear having a pack of cards in the house because it is said to be devil worship.

TECHNIQUES OF CARTOMANCY

There is much amusement to be gained from the study of cartomancy, and although a great amount of knowledge can be gained, it cannot be denied that these playthings may well be able to predict the future. It is also well known that many educated men and women today have their futures told, just as others have done in the past.

When the clairvoyants of today take a pack of cards and proceed to read them, they are simply following the examples of their predecessors. Cartomancy is still considered to be a very popular art, but in the past it was combined with a knowledge of astrology. Nowadays, the common practice is to follow the general rules laid down by one or two famous cartomancers and to rely upon intuition and experience for details.

Anyone with the slightest knowledge of clairvoyance is aware that sympathy with the enquirer is essential, for sometimes unpleasant events are indicated, for example the death of a loved one. For sceptics, the cards may be nothing more than a plaything. However, using them to predict the future may help in dealing with problems that arise in daily life.

As most cards have more than one meaning, to make a successful prediction it is important to look for a common factor. Also the meanings of some cards may change depending on their position and the influence of others around them.

In the following pages I have given several methods of making predictions by the cards, as well as a list of their separate meanings. In some of the methods I have reduced the normal pack of 52 playing cards to 36 cards by removing most of the cards with a value of less than 7; this makes readings quicker and easier. The pack of 36 cards consists of the following: 4 Aces, 4 Kings, 4 Queens, 4 Jacks, 4 Tens, 4 Nines, 4 Eights, 4 Sevens, 6 of Hearts, 4 of Hearts, 3 of Hearts, 2 of Hearts.

After a list of each card's separate meaning, I have included two other lists — one for combinations of cards and the other for groups of cards with the same numerical value.

When you first try to follow the methods described in this book, your readings will be hesitant and mechanical, but as the cards become more familiar you will become much more proficient.

The Ritual

The most important thing about card-reading is to take your time. Never attempt to read the cards hurriedly. Remember that card-reading was brought to its peak by the Gipsies, who believe in taking their time in reading cards, and if you are going to enjoy the art you will probably get far better results if you are relaxed. In fact the whole process works best when both the reader and the enquirer are totally relaxed.

Another very important factor is to choose the right pack of cards. You will find that a souvenir pack will give the best results for it tends to hold a special aura of its own.

The Signifier

When reading the cards it is important that an enquirer be signified by one of the 12 court cards that best suits his or her description.

Once this court card, known as the signifier, has been selected from the pack it should be placed in front of the area where the rest of the cards are to be laid. This should be done before shuffling and cutting the pack.

Shuffling and Cutting

The enquirer should shuffle the pack and be satisfied that it has been done thoroughly. He or she should then cut the pack with the left hand into three separate piles, moving to the left, as shown in the diagram above opposite.

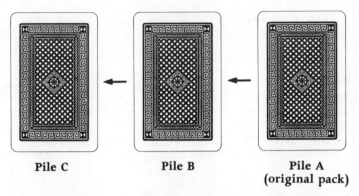

Pile C   Pile B   Pile A
(original pack)

After this the reader should turn each separate pile over so that
the bottom card of each pile is face up, as below.

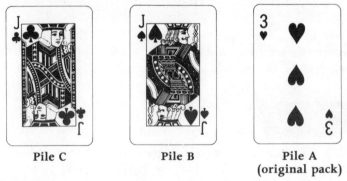

Pile C   Pile B   Pile A
(original pack)

After completing this the reader should make a prediction, for
these three cards (in this example, the Jack of Clubs, Jack of
Spades and 3 of Hearts) show the immediate influence that the
enquirer is under at the time of the reading. Once this is
completed the reader should turn each pile back to its original
position, as shown below.

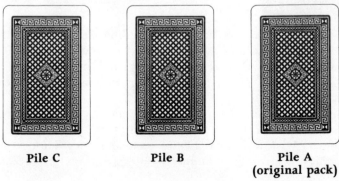

Pile C   Pile B   Pile A
(original pack)

The enquirer should then rebuild the pack, once again using the left hand and moving towards the left, as shown in the diagram below.

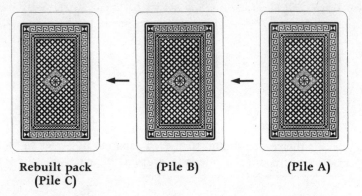

Rebuilt pack   **(Pile B)**   **(Pile A)**
(Pile C)

If any cards are dropped while being shuffled the prediction or meaning they contain will take place within 24 hours or during that week.

Wishing

While shuffling the pack of cards the enquirer can make a wish. The first card that appears in the reading is said to give the answer to the wish. However, this answer may not always be what the enquirer is hoping to hear, so care must be taken in analysing the answer, taking into account the enquirer's feelings.

Reading

You are now ready to begin your reading. Study the cards as they fall and interpret them as they strike your intuition. Once you start to read regularly the meanings and interpretations will come naturally, giving you a better and more spontaneous reading.

You will have lots of fun as you delight your friends with predictions from the cards that actually come true.

If you wish to become highly proficient you should keep a notebook with your own special interpretations of the cards.

Remember that you cannot expect to become a specialist overnight — this can take quite a long time and a good deal of patience and will depend on your own level of intuition. However you can have lots of fun right from the start of your very first reading. Also, it is comforting to know that you will never again be stuck for something to do if a party ever becomes drab and boring.

Variations

The method of reading described above is the one used by most clairvoyants. There are, however, other methods. For example, some clairvoyants believe that the top card of each pile gives additional information about the enquirer's immediate future. Others believe that Pile A represents the enquirer's past, Pile B his or her present influence and Pile C the future. Occasionally, a clairvoyant will ask the enquirer to select one of the three piles (A, B or C) and then concentrate the entire reading on this pile, rather than have the pack rebuilt.

INTERPRETATIONS
OF EACH CARD

There are two ways of explaining the cards individually — one makes use of the 52 card pack and the other uses the 36 card pack, discarding most of the cards with a value less than seven, the exceptions being the 2, 3, 4 and 6 of Hearts. The former is said to be the English method, which does not include the reverse meanings of the cards, as 104 meanings are considered to be too many to remember.

The latter system is more easily traced to the Gipsies and in it the cards have a reversed meaning as well as an original meaning.

The following interpretations apply to the 52 card pack and have been derived from the traditional and modern sources of knowledge. However, since the art of cartomancy has been passed down through many ages and many lands, it must be remembered that the interpretations have been handed down from generation to generation by word of mouth.

The interpretations that appear in this book are based upon one of the oldest systems known and have been altered slightly because of some of the more modern meanings in use today.

(The phrase "period of" refers to a number of days, weeks, months or years until, or the month of the year in which, a prediction is likely to be fulfilled. For example, a period of 6 could mean six days, six weeks, six months, six years or the sixth month, being June.)

ERROR The Publishers advise that the meanings of all Heart and Diamond cards on pages 16-22 and pages 24-27 have been inadvertently transposed. Thus, for example, the Ace of Diamonds on page 16 should mean "a piece of jewellery, a wedding or an engagement", while the Ace of Hearts should mean "the home or domestic situation". The Publishers apologise for any inconvenience that this might cause.

A ♣ ♦ ♥ ♠

News in the form of
a letter or telephone
call

A piece of jewellery,
a wedding or an
engagement

The home or
domestic situation

A government
building

K ♣ ♦ ♥ ♠

A middle-aged man
with brown eyes
and whose hair is
more dark than fair

A middle-aged man
with blue, grey or
green eyes and
blonde, red or grey
hair

A middle-aged man
with hazel eyes and
whose hair is more
fair than dark

A middle-aged man
with dark eyes,
dark hair and a dark
complexion

A female of any age with brown eyes and whose hair is more dark than fair

A female of any age with grey or green eyes and blonde, red or grey hair

A female of any age with hazel or green eyes and whose hair is more fair than dark

A female of any age with dark eyes, dark hair and a dark complexion

A male up to the age of 25 with brown eyes and whose hair is more dark than fair

A male up to the age of 25 with light eyes and fair hair

A male up to the age of 25 with hazel or green eyes and whose hair is more fair than dark

A male up to the age of 25 with dark eyes, dark hair and dark complexion

10 ♣ ♦ ♥ ♠

Travel, within the country, or overseas; period of 10

A large sum of money; period of 10

A good omen; period of 10

News of hospital treatment (possibly a serious illness); period of 10

9 ♣ ♦ ♥ ♠

Successful results; period of 9

A surprise gift; period of 9

Your wish will come true; period of 9

Delays and disappointments; period of 9

Discussions; period of 8

Changes; period of 8

News about work; period of 8

News of legal papers; period of 8

Family members; period of 7

Good results (studies or legal transactions); period of 7

A successful new idea; period of 7

Mild illness; an argument; period of 7

19

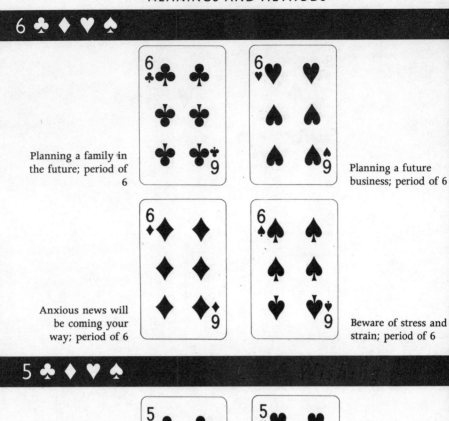

6 ♣ ♦ ♥ ♠

Planning a family in the future; period of 6

Planning a future business; period of 6

Anxious news will be coming your way; period of 6

Beware of stress and strain; period of 6

5 ♣ ♦ ♥ ♠

Deep thought leading to success; period of 5

Doing a business course; period of 5

Troubles around a relationship; period of 5

Deep concerns; period of 5

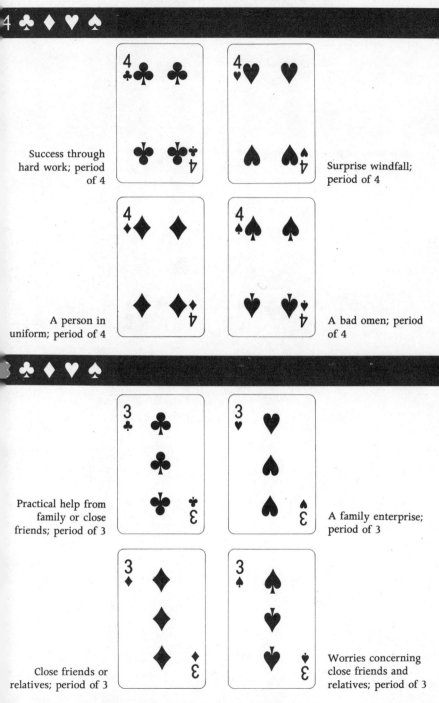

Success through
hard work; period
of 4

Surprise windfall;
period of 4

A person in
uniform; period of 4

A bad omen; period
of 4

Practical help from
family or close
friends; period of 3

A family enterprise;
period of 3

Close friends or
relatives; period of 3

Worries concerning
close friends and
relatives; period of 3

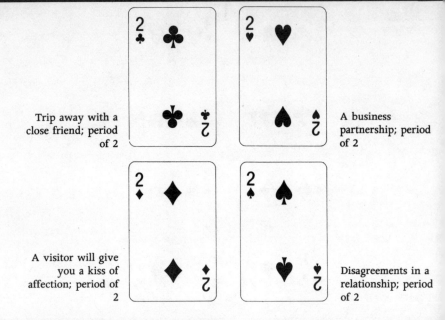

Trip away with a close friend; period of 2

A business partnership; period of 2

A visitor will give you a kiss of affection; period of 2

Disagreements in a relationship; period of 2

THE 36 CARD PACK

The practice of using a pack of 36 cards, as previously mentioned, is to simplify the readings. Also, with only 36 cards, the reading becomes slightly quicker. This method, as mentioned before, was traced back to the Eastern countries and used mainly by the Gipsies.

The 36 card pack consists of the following cards: 4 Aces, 4 Kings, 4 Queens, 4 Jacks, 4 Tens, 4 Nines, 4 Eights, 4 Sevens, 6 of Hearts, 4 of Hearts, 3 of Hearts, 2 of Hearts.

In the following pages I have listed the interpretations for these cards as they differ slightly in meaning to the entire pack of 52 cards.

Special care should be taken when using the pack of 36 cards because their interpretation will depend on whether they fall upright or reversed. The meanings of the two positions may be totally different.

In days gone by it was easier to recognise whether a card was upright or reversed. Nowadays, cards are designed in such a way that there is usually no right or wrong way up. It is necessary, therefore, to mark the cards you are going to use for fortune-telling to indicate to you the position in which they have fallen. These marks should be made before the pack is used and need not be changed if the cards are kept for the sole purpose of cartomancy.

In the following pages this selected pack is used for two methods of predicting the future.

Note: The interpretation for a reversed card is identified by the letter R preceding the description.

The phrase "period of" refers to a number of days, weeks, months or years until, or the month of the year in which, a prediction is likely to be fulfilled. For example, a period of 6 could mean six days, six weeks, six months, six years or the sixth month, being June.

A ♣ ♦ ♥ ♠

News in the form of
a letter or telephone
call

*R: Sudden news,
possibly leading to a
journey*

A piece of jewellery,
a wedding or
engagement

*R: Worries over a
piece of jewellery,
possibly a robbery*

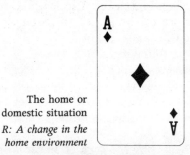

The home or
domestic situation

*R: A change in the
home environment*

A government
building

R: A severe illness

K ♣ ♦ ♥ ♠

A middle-aged male
with brown eyes
and whose hair is
more dark than fair

*R: A man of a
favourable
disposition with
possible business
connections; a dear
friend*

A middle-aged male
with blue, grey or
green eyes and
blonde, red or grey
hair

*R: A man connected
with the government
or a large enterprise*

A middle-aged male
with hazel eyes and
whose hair is more
fair than dark

*R: A man of charm,
possibly a confidence
trickster*

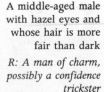

A middle-aged male
with dark eyes,
dark hair and dark
complexion

*R: A man of the law
(policeman, lawyer)*

A female of any age with brown eyes and whose hair is more dark than fair

R: A woman of a warm and friendly disposition, possibly a nurse, doctor or schoolteacher

A female of any age with grey or green eyes and blonde, red or grey hair

R: A woman interested in material wealth or an accountant

A female of any age, with hazel or green eyes and whose hair is more fair than dark

R: A flirtatious female

A female of any age with dark eyes, dark hair and a dark complexion

R: A widow; tears

A male up to the age of 25, with brown eyes and whose hair is more dark than fair

R: A dark-haired male friend or young bachelor

A male up to the age of 25 with light eyes and fair hair

R: News of a male accountant or bank manager

A male up to the age of 25 with hazel or green eyes and whose hair is more fair than dark

R: A male solicitor or news from a good friend

A male up to the age of 25 with dark eyes, dark hair and a dark complexion

R: A devious young bachelor

10 ♣ ♦ ♥ ♠

Travel, either within the country or overseas; period of 10

R: Letters from friends or family at a distance, within the country or overseas

A large sum of money; period of 10

R: Investments or a transfer of funds

A good omen; period of 10

R: Any existing problems will soon be solved

News of hospital treatment (possibly a serious illness); period of 10

R: A bad omen

9 ♣ ♦ ♥ ♠

Successful results; period of 9

R: Promotion at work; news of a new job or line of work

A surprise gift; period of 9

R: Lending or borrowing of money

Your wish will soon come true; period of 9

R: A surprise windfall

Delays and disappointments; period of 9

R: A serious or long-term illness

8 ♣ ♦ ♥ ♠

Discussions; period of 8

R: Worries around a health problem, possibly related to alcohol

Changes; period of 8

R: A change for the better

News about work; period of 8

R: An important decision to be made

News of legal papers; period of 8

R: Journey by car or train; possible change of residence

7 ♣ ♦ ♥ ♠

Family members; period of 7

R: A large gathering of people with a common interest, possibly a club or an amusement parlour

Good results (studies or legal transactions); period of 7

R: Paperwork

A successful new idea; period of 7

R: News of someone interested in art or clairvoyancy

Mild illness; an argument; period of 7

R: News of an operation

6 4 3 2 ♥

Anxious news will
be coming your
way; period of 6

R: A discovery

A person in
uniform; period of 4

*R: Relationship
problems*

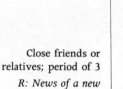

Close friends or
relatives; period of 3

*R: News of a new
acquaintance*

A visitor will give
you a kiss of
affection; period of
2

*R: A new baby; a
birth*

CARDS IN COMBINATION

As we already know, each suit of the cards has different meaning, for instance Clubs refer to business and success, Hearts refer to the emotions, Diamonds refer to material wealth and Spades are an ill omen. However, when these suits are combined they are influenced by the other cards in the lay. For example, if a Spade were to appear with a Club, the overall outcome would not be as bad as all Spades together.

When reading the cards there are some that quite often fall together. In the following pages I have provided a list of these cards and their combined interpretations.

A♣ and

5 of Clubs	A letter or phone call from an intellectual friend
4 of Clubs	News of a labourer
10 of Diamonds	News of a legacy
2 of Diamonds	A gift of flowers
8 of Spades	News of a traffic infringement
7 of Spades	A warning to take care around the home
6 of Spades	News of a person of a nervous disposition
3 of Spades	News of a mild illness

A♥ and

10 of Diamonds	Real estate, investment
7 of Diamonds	A correspondence course
9 of Hearts	Buying a first home
8 of Hearts	A real estate agent
7 of Hearts	Redecorating a home
4 of Hearts	Welfare housing

A ♦ and

9 of Diamonds	A surprise announcement
10 of Hearts	Engagement which will lead to marriage
9 of Hearts	A perfectly matched couple
3 of Hearts	A childhood lover
2 of Hearts	A new romance
8 of Spades	A wedding certificate

A ♠ and

9 of Clubs	A compensation claim
8 of Hearts	A government worker, possibly someone connected with social welfare
4 of Hearts	Member of the armed forces
2 of Hearts	A birth certificate or adoption papers
10 of Spades	Prison, trouble with the law
8 of Spades	A gift of land, or a will

10 ♣ and

8 of Hearts	A job that requires a lot of travel
7 of Hearts	A journey to somewhere new
4 of Hearts	A travelling government official
2 of Hearts	A lover who travels frequently
10 of Spades	Injury through a car accident
7 of Spades	Travel sickness

10 ♥ and

4 of Hearts	Good results in dealings with the law

10 ♦ and

9 of Diamonds	A gift of money; an unexpected inheritance
9 of Clubs	A lottery win

10 ♠ and

8 of Hearts	One who works with medical equipment or supplies, possibly a chemist
4 of Hearts	Someone who works for a hospital, possibly a nurse or doctor
8 of Spades	A medical document
7 of Spades	Someone who needs continual medical treatment

9♣ and
3 of Hearts   A family reunion

9♦ and
8 of Hearts   A jeweller
3 of Hearts   A gift to be sent in the mail
8 of Spades   Insurance papers

8♣ and
8 of Hearts   News of a contractor or contracts to be signed

8♥ and
3 of Hearts   An office party

7♣ and
7 of Diamonds and 3 of Hearts   A family tree being traced

The following combinations of cards foretell death:
Ace of Spades reversed and the *10 of Spades*
Ace of Spades reversed; with the *9 of Spades* and the *Queen of Spades*

INTERPRETATIONS
OF CARD GROUPS

When reading the cards, quite often several cards of the same value fall together. When this happens, each group of cards has a special meaning. The following list gives the meanings of cards of the same value:

Four Aces   A new life
Four Kings   A large corporation or enterprise
Four Queens   Evil gossip
Four Jacks   Mischief or trouble
Four 10s   A successful business venture
Four 9s   Large and unexpected windfall or surprise
Four 8s   A sudden change which will bring happiness
Four 7s   An unexpected arrival of a visitor to the home
Four cards of values less than 7   A certainty of success
Three Aces   A successful family enterprise
Three Kings   A visit to a large government building
Three Queens   Tea or bridge party
Three Jacks   A visit to a large office building
Three 10s   An important change is about to take place
Three 9s   Sudden and unexpected news
Three 8s   Signing of papers over a new enterprise
Three 7s   News of an unexpected birth
Three cards of values less than 7   A relative may enter a government post
Two Aces   News of an old acquaintance
Two Kings   A business discussion
Two Queens   A friend is in trouble
Two Jacks   A bachelors' party
Two 10s   A block of land may be acquired
Two 9s   A change in address; a new car
Two 8s   An unexpected romance
Two 7s   An unexpected invitation from a friend
Two cards of values less than 7   A young person may visit the home; a small journey

Some interesting facts about the cards

Those who are interested in the study of cartomancy will find the following facts intriguing. You can decide for youself whether or not they have any special significance.

The 52 cards in the pack coincide with the 52 weeks of the year.

The 13 cards in each suit coincide with the 13 lunar months and the 13 weeks in each quarter.

There are four suits, just as there are four seasons in the year, four periods during the day (morning, noon, afternoon and night), and humans have four stages of growth (childhood, teenage, adulthood and old age).

The 12 court cards in the pack coincide with the 12 months of the year and the 12 zodiac signs.

PAST, PRESENT AND FUTURE

here is a very easy method of studying the past, present and future by the cards. For this, the pack of 36 cards is normally used. Once the signifying card has been removed, the pack should be cut in the usual way (shuffle, then cut with the left hand into three piles, moving from right to left), but it should not then be rebuilt because each pile is used to tell the enquirer's life history.

The pile on the left-hand side of the reader is the past; the pile in the centre is the present and the pile on the right is the future, as shown below.

The signifying card

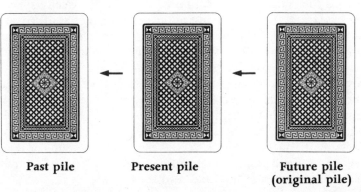

Past pile	Present pile	Future pile (original pile)

The Pathfinder

Before the reading can begin, the top card of each pile must be used to form a separate group, called "the pathfinder". This group is read first because it indicates the influence that the enquirer has around him at the present time, as shown below.

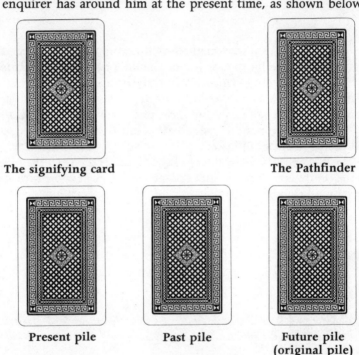

The signifying card   The Pathfinder

Present pile   Past pile   Future pile
                                            (original pile)

If, for example, a dark-haired, dark-complexioned 20-year-old male is the enquirer, he must be signified in the usual way, i.e. by the Jack of Spades. The rest of the cards are then shuffled and cut by the enquirer to form three piles, representing the past, present and future. Once this has been done the pathfinder must be formed. Suppose that the cards are as follows: King of Clubs, reversed; 9 of Clubs and 8 of Clubs. From this we can say that at the present time he is influenced by a successful business discussion that has recently taken place with a middle-aged male with brown hair and hazel eyes.

As the normal practice is to read the cards in groups of four, when reading the past, present and future, we shall lay each pile down into groups of four and read them.

The Reading

The Past

Queen of Spades   A dark-haired, dark-eyed female
King of Diamonds   A fair-haired, middle-aged male with light
                        eyes
7 of Spades   A mild illness
10 of Clubs   A journey, possibly overseas

From these four cards we can say that the enquirer went on a journey to visit a dark-haired female and a fair-haired male, and while on this journey he suffered a slight ailment.

6 of Hearts   Anxious news
10 of Hearts   A good omen
7 of Hearts   A new idea
Ace of Clubs, reversed   Sudden news, phone call or letter

The enquirer received some anxious news, either by phone or letter, which was to bring him good luck and incorporated some of his new ideas.

9 of Diamonds   A surprise
King of Hearts   A middle-aged male, more fair than dark, with
                     hazel eyes
Queen of Hearts   A female with fair hair and hazel eyes
Ace of Hearts   The home

A fair-haired, middle-aged couple gave the enquirer a surprise invitation to come and stay at their home.

Ace of Spades, reversed   A serious illness
4 of Hearts   A uniformed person

In the past, the enquirer has received news about a person who normally wears a uniform having a serious illness. (In the situation where less than four cards remain, the reader should continue and interpret them as they appear.)

The Present

Queen of Clubs   A female, more dark than fair, with brown
                     eyes.
8 of Spades   Legal papers
Jack of Diamonds   A male up to the age of 25 with blue eyes and
                        red or fair hair
9 of Hearts   The wish card

This signifies that the enquirer is waiting for some news of a legal paper that concerns a wish of his. However, at the moment this legal paper is in the hands of a female with dark hair and brown eyes and a male with blue eyes and fair hair.

7 of Diamonds, reversed Paperwork
9 of Spades Delays and disappointments
King of Spades A middle-aged male with dark eyes and dark hair
7 of Clubs, reversed A group of people with the same interest
The enquirer is presently waiting for news concerning some paperwork that has been delayed by a middle-aged male with dark eyes and dark hair who has the same interests as himself.

Jack of Hearts A male up to the age of 25 with fair eyes and hazel or green hair
2 of Hearts Affectionate welcome
A young male with fair hair and fair eyes will greet the enquirer warmly.

The Future
Queen of Diamonds A female with blue or green eyes and red or fair hair
10 of Spades A hospital
3 of Hearts Close relatives or friends
Ace of Diamonds A piece of jewellery; a wedding or engagement
The enquirer may propose to a female with blue or green eyes and red or fair hair, possibly a nurse or doctor, who is already a close friend.

8 of Hearts The work card
10 of Diamonds A large sum of money
Jack of Clubs A male under the age of 25 with hair more dark than fair, and brown eyes
8 of Diamonds Changes (business or home)
This indicates that the enquirer will enter into a business partnership with a male who is more dark than fair and who has brown eyes.

ASTROLOGY BY THE CARDS

This method requires the pack of 52 cards, which must be shuffled and cut in the normal way (remove the signifying card first, and then shuffle the remainder of the pack thoroughly. After this, cut the pack with the left hand into three separate piles, moving from right to left, as below.)

The signifying card

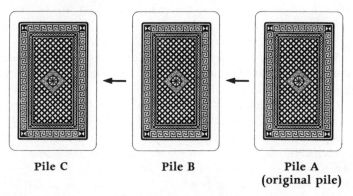

Pile C	Pile B	Pile A (original pile)

After the pack has been shuffled and cut, each separate pile should be turned over for the first prediction, which is made from the three bottom cards and is known as the "immediate influence", as shown overleaf.

The signifying card

Bottom Card	Bottom Card	Bottom Card
Pile C	Pile B	Pile A
		(original pile)

Once this has been done the pack should be rebuilt in the usual way. In other words, turn the cards over and, using the left hand, put the three piles one on top of each other, working from right to left. Leave the signifying card where it is.

After the pack has been rebuilt, the enquirer may then make a wish. The first card that appears in the reading is said to give the answer to the wish.

The cards should then be laid out in twelve horizontal rows of four, with a final row of three cards.

Separate readings of each row of cards should then be made, interpreting the cards according to the meanings given in the chapter "Interpretations of Each Card". In addition, however, the Aces and number cards are used to indicate the month of the year, or the zodiac sign, as shown in the table opposite.

In the following pages we will suppose that the enquirer is a fair-haired young bachelor with blue eyes. The signifying card will therefore be the Jack of Hearts. After shuffling and cutting the cards, the reading can begin.

MONTH	CARD	ZODIAC SIGN
January	ACE	Capricorn or Aquarius
February	TWO	Aquarius or Pisces
March	THREE	Pisces or Aries
April	FOUR	Aries or Taurus
May	FIVE	Taurus or Gemini
June	SIX	Gemini or Cancer
July	SEVEN	Cancer or Leo
August	EIGHT	Leo or Virgo
September	NINE	Virgo or Libra
October	TEN	Libra or Scorpio
November	TWO ACES	Scorpio or Sagittarius
December	TWO AND TEN	Sagittarius or Capricorn

The Immediate Influence

King of Spades A middle-aged male with very dark hair and eyes and a dark complexion

10 of Spades News of hospital treatment; someone born in October or under the signs of Scorpio or Libra

9 of Clubs Quick success

This indicates that the enquirer will receive news of a middle-aged male with a dark complexion, born in the month of October or under the sign of Scorpio or Libra, who will need some hospital treatment and will have a quick recovery.

The Reading

6 of Clubs A family in the future; month of June

3 of Hearts Close friends or relatives

3 of Spades Concerns around close friends or relatives

7 of Diamonds   Good results around studies or legal transactions

This signifies that in the month of June the enquirer will have
some worries concerning close relatives or friends who may be
involved in a legal transaction.

5 of Diamonds   Business course studies; month of May
7 of Spades   Slight illness
10 of Diamonds   A large sum of money
3 of Clubs   Practical help from family and friends

In the month of May there will be news of a possibly wealthy
relative becoming ill.

Ace of Diamonds   Jewellery, engagement or wedding; month of
January
8 of Hearts   The work card
10 of Spades   A hospital
Ace of Clubs   News

The enquirer will be invited to a wedding in the month of
January by somebody who works in the medical profession.

9 of Diamonds   A surprise; month of September
King of Diamonds   A middle-aged male with blonde hair and
blue eyes
7 of Hearts   A new idea
Queen of Diamonds   A female with red hair and light eyes

In the month of September the enquirer will receive a surprise
business idea from a fair-haired, middle-aged couple.

Jack of Diamonds   A male up to the age of 25 with light eyes
and fair hair
King of Hearts   A middle-aged male with hazel eyes and fair
hair
Queen of Spades   A female with dark eyes and hair
8 of Clubs   Discussions; month of August

In August there will be a discussion, probably on a business
basis, with a young, fair-haired male and a middle-aged couple.

2 of Clubs   A trip away with a close friend
5 of Hearts   Worries about a relationship; month of May
King of Clubs   A middle-aged male with brown eyes and dark
hair

10 of Hearts   A good omen; month of October; Libra
   In the month of May the enquirer will be going on a trip with a Libran male who is a close friend.

Queen of Clubs   A female with brown eyes and dark hair
Jack of Spades   A male up to the age of 25 with very dark hair and eyes
9 of Clubs   Quick success; month of September; Virgo
Jack of Clubs   A male up to the age of 25 with brown eyes, and who is more dark than fair
   There will be news from a dark-haired couple about the success of a young dark-haired bachelor born under the sign of Virgo.

4 of Spades   A bad card; month of April
Queen of Hearts   A female with fair hair and green eyes
Ace of Spades   A government building; Capricorn or Pisces; month of January
7 of Clubs   A family member, period of 7
   The enquirer is in danger of a jealous fair-haired woman who works for the government and is born under the sign of Capricorn or Pisces.

King of Spades   A middle-aged male with dark hair
6 of Hearts   Anxious news; month of June; Gemini or Cancer
5 of Spades   Deep concern
4 of Hearts   A person in uniform
   There will be news of a middle-aged male connected with the law and born under the sign of Gemini or Cancer who will cause the enquirer deep concern.

9 of Spades   Delays and disappointments; month of September
3 of Diamonds   A family enterprise
5 of Clubs   Success through deep thought
4 of Clubs   Success through hard work
   The enquirer is involved in a family enterprise which could suffer a setback in the month of September but will be corrected with a lot of deep thought and hard work.

Ace of Hearts   The home; domestic situations; month of January
8 of Diamonds   Changes

2 of Spades   Relationship worries
4 of Diamonds   A surprise windfall
   In January there will be relationship worries and changes for the enquirer because of a surprise windfall.

10 of Clubs   A journey, either within the country or overseas; month of October
6 of Spades   Beware of stress and strain
8 of Spades   Legal papers
2 of Hearts   A kiss of affection
   In October there will be news of legal papers, from a distant town or city, causing the enquirer stress, strain and worries over a loved one.

6 of Diamonds   A business in the future; month of June
2 of Diamonds   A business partnership
9 of Hearts   The wish card
   In the month of June the enquirer will be entering into a business partnership connected with one of his heart's desires.

DELLA'S METHOD

This method of cartomancy, in which the pack of 36 cards is used, uses a four-card layout. It is one of the easiest to understand and is very simple and straightforward.

The pack should be cut and shuffled in the usual way and then divided into three groups, as before. Once this has been done the packs are then turned over, with the bottom cards face upwards. Our first prediction is then made since these three cards are said to hold the influence that the enquirer is under (*see* Shuffling and Cutting, pp. 11–12). When this has been done the packs are turned back to their original positions and then rebuilt.

The enquirer must be signified in the usual manner, but the signifying card should be left in the pack. The cards are then dealt out in groups of four, one group at a time.

In the following pages I have included a sample reading, the enquirer being a young, dark-haired, green-eyed female, signified by the Queen of Clubs.

The Immediate Influence

8 of Clubs   Discussions; period of 8
Queen of Hearts   A female with fair hair and blue eyes
9 of Diamonds   A surprise gift
There will be a surprise gift for the enquirer from a fair-haired, blue-eyed female in a period of 8

The Reading

Ace of Spades, reversed   A serious illness
King of Diamonds   A business
King of Hearts   A fair-haired man with green eyes
7 of Spades   A slight illness; period of 7

There will be news of a fair-haired businessman having a serious illness in a period of 7.

King of Spades, reversed   A man of the law
7 of Hearts   A new idea; period of 7
Jack of Spades   A male up to the age of 25 with very dark hair and eyes
Queen of Spades   A female with dark hair and eyes
The enquirer will be hearing news of a dark-haired couple having dealings with the law, in a period of 7.

9 of Diamonds   A surprise; period of 9
Ace of Hearts, reversed   Changes to the home
2 of Hearts, reversed   A new baby
Ace of Diamonds   An engagement, wedding or piece of jewellery
There will be news of an unexpected baby and a piece of jewellery in a period of 9.

8 of Spades   Legal papers
Queen of Diamonds   A red-haired female with hazel eyes
Ace of Clubs   News by mail or phone
7 of Diamonds   Good results; period of 7
There will be news of good results around legal papers being dealt with by a red-haired female in a period of 7.

3 of Hearts   Close friends or relatives; period of 3
9 of Clubs   Quick success
8 of Hearts   Thw work card
7 of Clubs, reversed   A group of people with the same interests
A family enterprise that the enquirer is involved in will be successful in a period of 3.

Queen of Hearts   A fair-haired, blue-eyed female
King of Clubs   A dark-haired, middle-aged male, brown eyes
Jack of Diamonds   A brown-haired male up to the age of 25
Jack of Clubs   A black-haired male up to the age of 25
There will be a large celebration centred around the enquirer.

10 of Hearts ⎫
10 of Spades ⎬   An important change
10 of Clubs ⎭ (Injury through a car accident)
Jack of Hearts, reversed   News from a solicitor or friend
   There is good news from a solicitor about an injury caused by a car accident.

10 of Diamonds   A large sum of money
9 of Hearts   The wish card; period of 9
8 of Clubs   Discussions
Queen of Clubs   The enquirer
   The enquirer will be involved in discussions about a large sum of money in a period of 9.

YOUR DESTINY IN 52 CARDS

The following method uses the pack of 52 cards and is fairly easy to understand. Remove the signifier and shuffle and cut the pack in the usual way. After the pack has been cut and divided into its usual three piles, the first prediction is made, using the bottom card of each pile, because these cards indicate the immediate influence that surrounds the enquirer. Each separate pile should be returned to its normal position and the top card of each pile must then be placed on the signifier. This group now becomes known as the pathfinder, for it indicates the path the enquirer should follow. Once this is completed the pack should be rebuilt, except for the pathfinder, which remains out of the pack.

Now, lay out the first 12 cards, face down, in three horizontal rows of four. This process must be repeated until there are twelve groups of four cards. When this is completed, go back to the pathfinder, the group that contains the signifier, and begin reading the signifier's destiny. Continue with the 12 other groups of cards.

This method of predicting somebody's destiny can cover a period from the immediate future to a span of five years.

In the following example a bachelor of the age of 22 with hazel eyes and dark brown hair is the enquirer; therefore, he is signified by the Jack of Clubs.

The Immediate Influence

Jack of Spades A male up to the age of 25 with very dark hair and eyes
5 of Clubs Success through deep thought
3 of Clubs Practical help from close friends and family

The enquirer will receive news of a person who needs some practical help, possibly a brother.

The Pathfinder

Jack of Clubs   The enquirer
6 of Diamonds   A future business
2 of Spades   Relationship worries
5 of Diamonds   A business course; period of 5
   The enquirer is doing a course in business studies. He is concerned about a relationship but everything will be solved in a period of 5.

The Reading

5 of Spades   Deep concern
3 of Spades   Concern about close friends or family
3 of Diamonds   A family enterprise
2 of Diamonds   A business partnership; period of 2
   In a period of 2 there will be deep concern about a family enterprise.

7 of Diamonds   Good results; paperwork
Ace of Hearts   The home or domestic situation
Queen of Spades   A female with very dark hair and eyes
4 of Clubs   Success through hard work; period of 4
   There will be news of a female with very dark hair and eyes relating to paperwork in connection with a house. Any problems will be solved through hard work and deep thought in a period of 4.

10 of Diamonds   A large sum of money
Queen of Diamonds   A brown-haired female with hazel eyes
Jack of Diamonds   A male up to the age of 25 with light hair and eyes
6 of Spades   Beware of stress and strain
   A large sum of money will be causing worries and stress to a fair-haired couple.

Ace of Diamonds   A wedding, engagement or piece of jewellery
6 of Clubs   A future family
10 of Spades   A hospital
7 of Hearts   A new idea; period of 7
   There will be news to the enquirer of a wedding in a period of

7 connected with a person in the medical profession.

Jack of Spades   A male up to the age of 25 with very dark hair and eyes
King of Hearts   A middle-aged male with hazel eyes and grey hair
10 of Clubs   A journey of some distance, possibly overseas
6 of Hearts   Anxious news; period of 6
   In a period of 6 there will be anxious news from a male under the age of 25 with very dark hair and eyes about a middle-aged male with hazel eyes and grey hair, who lives some distance away.

4 of Diamonds   A surprise windfall
4 of Hearts   A person in uniform; period of 4
King of Clubs   A middle-aged male with brown hair and green eyes
9 of Hearts   The wish card
   In a period of 4 the enquirer will be sharing a surprise windfall with a middle-aged male with brown hair and green eyes.

9 of Spades   Delays and disappointments
3 of Hearts   Close friends or relatives
Ace of Spades   Government or official business
9 of Diamonds   A surprise; period of 9
   There will be delayed news for the enquirer's relatives who are involved in some official dealings; however, everything will be resolved in a period of 9.

8 of Spades   Legal papers
Jack of Hearts   A fair-haired male under the age of 25; a solicitor
3 of Clubs   Practical help from family or friends; period of 3
10 of Hearts   A good omen
   The enquirer will receive good news concerning paperwork that is being dealt with by a solicitor, in a period of 3.

Queen of Hearts   A female with hazel eyes and blonde hair
King of Diamonds   A middle-aged male with green eyes and fair hair
7 of Clubs   The family
8 of Hearts   The work card; period of 8

In a period of 8 there will be news for the enquirer of a fair-haired couple, possibly his parents, going into business together.

2 of Hearts   Kiss of affection
8 of Diamonds   Changes
9 of Clubs   Quick success
4 of Spades   A bad omen; period of 4
In a period of 4 there will be changes made for the better in the enquirer's love life.

7 of Spades   A slight illness
2 of Clubs   A trip away with a close friend
5 of Clubs   Success through deep thought
8 of Clubs   Discussions; period of 8
After a slight illness the enquirer will think seriously about going away on a trip with a close friend; it will eventuate in a period of 8.

King of Spades   A middle-aged male with very dark hair and eyes
Ace of Clubs   News by letter or phone
5 of Hearts   Deep concern about a relationship
Queen of Clubs   A dark-haired woman with hazel eyes
There will be news of problems in a relationship concerning a dark-haired, middle-aged couple.

THE
ROMANY METHOD

In the following method the pack of 36 cards is used in a traditional way, said to have been passed down from the Gipsies. The pack is shuffled and cut in the usual manner with the enquirer's signifying card left in the pack.

Once the shuffling and cutting of the pack is completed and there are the usual three piles of cards, each pile is turned over so that the bottom card is face up. The first prediction can now be made to show the immediate influence surrounding the enquirer. After this has been done, each pile is turned back to its original position and the pack is rebuilt in the usual way.

After this, the reader should lay the first eight cards face down in two horizontal rows of four. This process should be repeated, layer upon layer until each pile in the top row of cards is five cards deep, and each pile in the bottom row of cards is four cards deep. You are now ready to begin the reading.

This method of predicting a person's future can cover a period from the present time to a span of nine months.

In the following example reading the enquirer is a young female with "mousy" brown hair and green eyes and is therefore signified by the Queen of Diamonds.

The Immediate Influence

9 of Clubs   Quick success; period of 9
8 of Hearts, reversed   An important decision to be made
10 of Spades   A hospital

Our enquirer is influenced by an important decision to be made regarding a hospital, possibly to do with an operation, in a period of 9.

The Reading

10 of Clubs   Travel — possibly overseas
King of Diamonds   A fair-haired, middle-aged male with green
eyes
Jack of Hearts, reversed   A solicitor; good news from a friend
8 of Clubs, reversed   Worries concerning a health problem.
Possible news of an alcoholic
King of Clubs, reversed   A man of good disposition, or a friend
There will be news from a fair-haired, middle-aged male,
possibly a solicitor, who lives some distance away and who has a
good disposition. He could possibly have a drinking problem.

Queen of Clubs, reversed   A friendly female, possibly a nurse,
teacher, or solicitor
King of Hearts   A middle-aged male with fair hair and hazel
eyes
Ace of Diamonds   An engagement, wedding or some jewellery
Jack of Diamonds   An accountant or bank manager
Jack of Spades   A bachelor's party
The enquirer will be invited to the wedding of a close friend,
possibly a nurse, who is marrying an accountant and the latter
will be having a bachelors party. The bride will be given away
by a middle-aged male with fair hair.

Queen of Diamonds, reversed   A female with monetary interests
3 of Hearts   Close friends or relatives; period of 3
6 of Hearts, reversed   A discovery
10 of Spades   A hospital
10 of Hearts   A block of land may be acquired
In a period of 3 the enquirer, a businesswoman involved with
the sale of land, will be making an interesting discovery about
hospital treatment.

9 of Clubs   Quick success
Ace of Hearts   The home or domestic situation
King of Spades, reversed   A man of the law
7 of Diamonds, reversed   Paperwork; period of 7
9 of Hearts, reversed   A surprise windfall
In a period of 7 the enquirer will be hearing sudden news
about a surprise windfall and she will consult her lawyer about
buying a home.

10 of Diamonds   A large sum of money
Ace of Clubs   News by letter or phone
9 of Diamonds, reversed   Lending or borrowing of money
9 of Spades   Delays and disappointments; period of 9
In a period of 9 the enquirer will be disappointed because of a large sum of money she is trying to borrow.

Ace of Spades, reversed   A serious illness
Queen of Hearts   A female with fair hair and blue eyes
7 of Clubs, reversed   A large gathering of people with the same interests
4 of Hearts, reversed   Relationship problems; period of 4
The enquirer will be invited to a large gathering of people, in a period of 4, by a fair-haired female who has a serious illness.

8 of Spades   Legal papers
2 of Hearts   Kiss of affection; period of 2
8 of Hearts, reversed   An important decision to be made
7 of Hearts, reversed   News of someone interested in art or clairvoyancy
In a period of 2 the enquirer will be hearing news of a artistic friend who will have to make an important decision concerning a legal paper.

8 of Diamonds   Changes
Jack of Clubs, reversed   A dark-haired friend or bachelor
7 of Spades   A mild illness
Queen of Spades, reversed   A widow or tears
The enquirer will have to change some plans because of news she will receive from a dark-haired bachelor about a widow with a mild illness.

QUESTIONS
AND ANSWERS

The following method of answering questions by cartomancy is very easily understood. The pack of 36 cards is used. The signifying card is removed and then the pack is cut and shuffled in the usual way. After this is done the pack should be rebuilt and the first four cards of the pack dealt out below the signifying card.

The first card dealt should signify to the reader the question in the enquirer's mind. The enquirer need not actually ask the question, simply concentrate on it.

After the first four cards have been dealt the rest of the pack is no longer needed and can be placed to one side.

The cards in the lay should immediately indicate what circumstances surround the enquirer and whether or not the answer will be to his or her liking.

Try to make a complete and comprehensive story out of the four cards in the lay, letting your intuition do the work. If, after laying out the cards, the question on the enquirer's mind is not answered, ask him or her if the cards have answered another question. It often happens that although a superficial question has not been answered, a deeper problem might have been revealed.

If the cards do not appear to have answered any questions, ask the enquirer to reshuffle the pack and begin again.

Some example questions and answers are given in the following pages:

Example 1
A young dark-haired bachelor with hazel eyes is worried about his girlfriend. The cards revealed the following:

Queen of Clubs, reversed   A female with a friendly disposition, could possibly be a nurse, doctor or teacher

8 of Hearts, reversed   An important decision is to be made

10 of Spades   A hospital; period of 10

10 of Hearts   A block of land might be acquired
Answer 1
I can see from the cards that you are concerned about a dark-haired female with a friendly disposition, possibly your girl-friend, who has an important decision to be made, probably about an operation. My advice to you is not to worry because I feel the operation will be a success and once that is over you will possibly acquire a block of land together.

Example 2
A blonde, blue-eyed female, about 22 years old, consulted the cards to know if there were any changes imminent in her life. The cards revealed the following:
8 of Diamonds   Changes; period of 8
6 of Hearts, reversed   A discovery
Jack of Diamonds, reversed   An accountant or bank manager
7 of Spades   A slight illness
Answer 2
I can see from the cards that your question is whether there are to be any immediate changes in your life. My answer is that you will soon be coming into contact with an accountant, bank manager, or someone in a similar profession, who will possibly become your boyfriend and who may have a slight illness in a period of 8.

Example 3
A middle-aged female with dark brown hair consulted the cards to find out whether or not she should take a holiday in the immediate future. The cards were as follows:
8 of Spades, reversed   A journey by car or train
King of Clubs, reversed   A businessman or a friend who has a favourable disposition
8 of Clubs, reversed   Worries around a health problem; possibly an alcoholic
8 of Hearts   An unexpected romance; period of 8
Answer 3
I can see from your cards that you are wondering whether or not to take a journey. I can safely tell you that you will be taking this journey in a period of 8 and that you will have an unexpected romance with a businessman of a favourable disposition who has a health problem.

Example 4
A dark-haired, dark-eyed 19-year-old bachelor consulted the cards to find out about a legal problem he was involved in. The cards were as follows:
8 of Spades   Legal papers
2 of Hearts   A kiss of affection; period of 2
Ace of Spades   A government or official building
10 of Clubs   A journey interstate or overseas
Answer 4
I can see from the cards that your question is about legal dealings. I can advise you that within a period of 2 you will be travelling some distance, possibly overseas, to deal with official business concerning this matter.

Example 5
A very dark-haired, brown-eyed, middle-aged male consulted the cards to ask about his wedding. The cards were as follows:
Ace of Diamonds   A wedding, engagement or piece of jewellery
8 of Diamonds, reversed   A change for the better
6 of Hearts   Anxious news
7 of Clubs   Family; period of 7
Answer 5
I see from your cards that you are asking about a wedding or possible engagement. My advice is that in a period of 7 there will be anxious news and a change for the better which will result in your wedding taking place.

Example 6
A middle-aged male with fair hair and green eyes consulted the cards to find out whether or not his wife was having extramarital affairs. The cards were as follows:
3 of Hearts, reversed   News of a new acquaintance
Queen of Hearts   A female with fair hair and blue eyes
Ace of Diamonds, reversed   Loss of a piece of jewellery
Jack of Diamonds, reversed   An accountant or bank manager
Answer 6
From these cards I can see that you are worried about a fair-haired female, possibly your wife. You feel that she has met somebody new. My answer to you is that she has met somebody new, a man who is younger than yourself and possibly a bank manager, and that she may leave you for him.

Example 7

A young, dark-haired female with dark brown eyes consulted the cards to find out if there would be any happiness on her future marriage.

10 of Hearts   A good omen
7 of Spades   A slight sickness
8 of Spades   Legal paper
2 of Hearts   A kiss of affection; period of 2

Answer 7

Your cards reveal that you are worried about future happiness. You will certainly have happiness in the future and you may be signing a legal paper in a period of 2, possibly a marriage certificate. However, I must caution you to take care of your health.

(*Note*: The 10 of Hearts specifically indicates the question about future happiness.)

PART II
FORTUNE-TELLING
GAMES

POETIC
FORTUNE-TELLING

This is a fairly easy party game in which the pack of 52 cards is shuffled and cut in the usual manner and then rebuilt. Then, one member of the group (the dealer) holds the pack and asks the other members to select one card each from the pack, using their left hand. The dealer then asks another member of the group to hold the pack while he or she draws a card, also using the left hand.

After everyone has selected a card the dealer reads the verse pertaining to each card, including his or her own.

A♣
The Ace of Clubs foretells
News by word
Or rings of bells.

A♦
The Ace of Diamonds tells
News of jewellery
Or wedding bells.

A♥
Now you have this Ace,
You shall soon be hearing
Of a new place.

A♠
With the Ace of Spades it is certain
You will soon be dealing with
Government persons.

K♣
The King of Clubs is trying to say
That a dark-haired man is coming your way.

K♦
As you have this card of the court:
From a fair-haired man, a visit or the sort.

K♥
The King of Hearts brings a surprise
From a fair-haired man with baby blue eyes.

K♠ You may hear news from a foreign port,
As you have this card of the court.

Q♣ The Queen of Clubs says
A meeting is there,
With a woman who looks
More dark than fair.

Q♦ Now that you are the holder of this Queen,
There will be news of a fair maiden with hair that
gleams.

Q♥ With the Queen of Hearts you shall soon sight
A green-eyed woman with hair that's light.

Q♠ You will soon be entering a foreign port,
As you have this Queen of the court.

J♣ The Jack of Clubs in your direction,
Is a man with a dark complexion.

J♦ With the Jack of Diamonds you are soon to sight
A man with a complexion that is light.

J♥ The one who draws the Jack of Hearts
Will soon meet a friend who likes the arts.

J♠ The Jack of Spades will find you caught
With a dark-haired person of similar thoughts.

10♣ For those of you who draw this Ten,
Prepare for travel with fellow men.

10♦ For those of you who like milk and honey,
Here comes a whole heap of money.

10♥ For those of you who deserve more,
Here comes the good you've always waited for.

10♠ For those who draw this Spade,
A hospital bed has been made!

9♣ For those of you who have been trying,
    Here comes Success — you'll soon be flying.

9♦ At this time you hold the Nine,
    A surprise will be yours, not mine.

9♥ If you've been feeling down and blue,
    A wish of yours will soon come true.

9♠ The Nine of Spades means to you
    Delays, and disappointments too.

8♣ This little Eight
    Foretells of a discussion
    With a mate.

8♦ A change of fate
    Will come your way
    From this Eight.

8♥ In the Eight of Hearts does lurk
    Changes connected with your work.

8♠ Now that you have this Spade,
    A legal paper will soon be made.

7♣ In the Seven of Clubs I foresee
    A family with changes to be.

7♦ With this little Seven,
    There will be good results from Heaven.

7♥ Now that you have the Seven of Hearts,
    You will soon have an idea of the Arts.

7♠ The Seven of Spades foretells
    Illnesses or evil spells.

6♣ In the Six of Clubs I foresee
    A family to be.

6 ♦ The Six of Diamonds tells
Of business spells.

6 ♥ No one alive is sufficiently smart
To escape the anxiety of the Six of Hearts.

6 ♠ The Six of Spades could bring much pain,
If you are not wary of stress and strain.

5 ♣ For success to be,
Deep thought
Is the advice from me.

5 ♦ Business studies are to be,
The Five of Diamonds is telling me.

5 ♥ If a lover is concerning you,
You should think deeply about what to do.

5 ♠ The Five of Spades is telling me
Deep concerns are soon to be.

4 ♣ The holder of this little Four
Will soon have to work more.

4 ♦ The Four of Diamonds tells me
Of a surprise windfall soon to be.

4 ♥ From this Four you may soon impress
A person in uniform dress.

4 ♠ If you draw the Four of Spades,
All your luck will soon fade.

3 ♣ Your problems will soon be at their ends,
With the help of your family or friends.

3 ♦ With the Three of Diamonds I foresee
A family enterprise to be.

3 ♥ Within a period of Three,
Close friends and relatives you shall see.

3♠ The Three of Spades is telling me
     Of anxiety around a family.

2♣ The holder of this little Two
     Will be having a trip too.

2♦ The Two of Diamonds is telling me
     Of a business partnership to be.

2♥ The Two of Hearts tells me,
     You shall soon be greeted affectionately.

2♠ Relationship worries are soon to be,
     The Two of Spades is telling me.

YOUR WEEK BY THE CARDS

Here is another easy and entertaining party game you can play using the pack of 52 cards.

The pack must be cut and shuffled as usual and then rebuilt. One member of the group (the dealer) holds the pack and asks the other members of the party to select one card each, using their left hand. The dealer then selects a card, also using the left hand, while another member of the party holds the pack.

The message pertaining to each card is given below:

You will receive news by phone or mail this week. You may have to make sudden plans to prepare for the unexpected. At work this week there may be news of a possible promotion, signing of legal papers or the satisfactory conclusion of a business deal. At home, there will be news of a marriage certificate, custody or adoption papers or a summons, all with good results, allowing you to plan for the future.

There will be news this week of an engagement or wedding. If you are engaged it is time to plan for your wedding. If you are married, there will be happy times ahead. For others, this card signifies the beginning of a relationship or deep friendship.

This week should be the week of co-operation around the home. For a young married couple this is the week to start planning for a home of their own. For those already established it can mean any of the following: renovations, unexpected visitors, a change in residence, a financial gain, unexpected news of a baby or a gift coming to the home.

Be prepared this week for government or official business. Be aware of traffic infringements, the loss of a loved one or a close friend through a serious illness. A week where obstacles may confront you; however, there will always be a way around them. This will be a week of hard work and possible strained relationships.

News from a friend with a pleasant personality or dealings with a brown-eyed male over the age of 25 who is more dark than fair. Also possible news from a business firm.

There will be news from a member of the government this week. Any decisions made this week will prove favourable. Also possible contact from a middle-aged male with light brown hair.

This is the week to be cautious, particularly of salesmen, and remember to check the small print before you sign anything. Also news of a middle-aged male with fair hair and light coloured eyes.

There will be problems to be solved this week, also dealings with the law. News of a middle-aged male with dark eyes and dark hair.

News from a female with brown eyes, who is more dark than fair, and who is a dear and true friend. Possible dealings this week with a woman who is a nurse, doctor or schoolteacher.

This week there will be a visit or phone call from a brown-haired female. Beware of false friends or enemies this week. You may hear from a businesswoman.

There will be news this week from a fair-haired female friend. Also possible dealings with a receptionist or a woman who works in an office.

Take care of your health this week because you may be plagued by a few minor ailments. This week may bring news of a widow or a strained relationship. You may also have dealings with a dark-complexioned female.

News from a dark, brown-haired male friend this week. There may be news of a bachelor's party.

This week brings contact with a male accountant or bank manager. You may hear from a young fair-haired male.

This week will bring contact from a male solicitor or a close male friend who lives some distance away. Also a meeting with a fair-haired, blue-eyed young man.

This week you will receive news from a foreign port or a town some distance away. There will be trouble from a very dark-haired male.

In the coming week there will be news of a trip that will take you either overseas or to a town some distance away. It will also bring news from friends and family whom you have not heard from for some time. Your intuition will be good this week and your lucky number is 7.

A lottery ticket or a large sum of money will be the centre of attention this week. This is the time to have a gamble and to consider some investments. Happy times are ahead.

A good week is ahead so be prepared for everything to fall into place. Your lucky number is 10.

This is a week when you should take better care of yourself. There could be news of a hospital, and a loved one might need hospital treatment this week.

A successful week ahead, so if you are applying for a job, seeking a wage rise or negotiating an important business deal, this is the week for it. Your lucky day is Monday and your lucky number is 9.

A week full of pleasant news, surprise gifts and invitations. Possible news of a coastal resort or a pleasant trip on the weekend.

This is the week when your dreams and desires just might come true. News of a birth and possible news from a lady friend, with pleasant results.

This week there will be disappointments, delays and trouble with transport. You may lose some money.

A neighbour or close friend may give you friendly advice this week. A favourable colour this week is white and lucky numbers are 5 and 8.

8 ♦

The week ahead will bring changes both at home and at work. Be prepared for something to go wrong with a car.

8 ♥

Your work will dominate the week — be prepared for a wage rise or promotion. Take things easy at the weekend.

8 ♠

A week of legal dealings. If you are waiting on an important document or applying for a licence this will be the week when it will happen.

7 ♣

This is the week to get out and about with the family and old friends. Possible news of a reunion.

7 ♦

A week where those things that you have been waiting for will eventuate, with good results. If you have been waiting on exam results or legal papers this is the time when you will hear. Best day of the week is Saturday.

7 ♥

A week in which to explore creative ideas and to redecorate your home. There will be changes on the work front. A week of happiness; your lucky numbers for the week are 7 and 9.

7 ♠

Be prepared for minor ailments this week. Take better care of your health and beware of any "fast foods" that you might eat this week. As there is a week of slight accidents ahead take extra care while travelling.

6 ♣

News of a baby this week. Also an invitation to a church gathering, possibly a christening or a wedding. Lucky number for the week is 3.

6 ♦

News of a successful small business venture, possibly within your own family, so be prepared for a garage sale. A week filled with happiness. Best day is Friday.

6 ♥

This week will be filled with anxiety so it is advisable not to plan anything permanent. Be prepared for slight disappointments and delays.

6 ♠

Beware of stress and strain this week. Don't lift anything heavy. The week will bring news of somebody with a nervous disposition. Try not to let minor disappointments get you down. Friday is an important day.

5 ♣

An emotional week ahead with worries concerning family and friends. Fate may bring a total change to your life.

5 ♦

A good week for business dealings. A time to get together with loved ones. Thursday may be an important day this week.

5 ♥

This is the week to take on something new. News of a baby boy. Lucky number for you this week is 5.

5 ♠

This week will be filled with worries and a feeling of getting nowhere fast. You will be tried and tested in every way.

4 ♣

You will have a lot of odd jobs to do this week but your efforts will be well worth the trouble because the outcome will be successful. Wednesday should be a good day both at home and at work.

4♦

A week full of pleasant little blessings; a small windfall might even come your way. A good week for studies and conferences or to consider taking on something new.

4♥

News of a person who wears a uniform. Be particularly careful about not breaking any laws this week. A good week to plan things for the rest of the year and for your future.

4♠

This could possibly be the worst week of the year. Evil influences will be at work and you will be pleased to see the end of it.

3♣

This will be your week to be a good Samaritan to your close friends and family, which will probably mean that you will not get anything done for yourself. However, there may be luck with a small bet; number 9 is the lucky number.

3♦

You may have to work extra hard this week. A small party might take place at home.

3♥

This is a week to be with close friends and family. Also time to plan that holiday with the loved ones.

3♠

This week there will be arguments at home and at work. A week to do things by yourself.

2♣

You might have to take a short journey with a close friend this week. Two pieces of pleasant news will come your way.

2 ♦

A small piece of jewellery might be the centre of attention this week. Monday is the best day of the week and your lucky numbers for the week are 2, 3, 6 and 23.

2 ♥

This week you will be greeted warmly everywhere you go. Old friends may reappear. Your ambitions may begin to be fulfilled.

2 ♠

There may be worries over a loved one's health this week. It is also a time when delays and frustrations might set you down. What you do this week will pay off next week.

PERSONALITIES
BY THE CARDS

I n this party game a pack of 40 cards is used including the number cards and the Aces but omitting the court cards. The pack should be shuffled and cut in the usual way. One member of the party (the dealer) holds the pack and asks the other members to select one card each. The dealer then selects a card while another member of the party holds the pack.

The personality traits of each participant will be indicated by the card that he or she has selected, as listed below.

The Ace of Clubs signifies that you are a very talkative person and that you have a tendency to become over-anxious. You are usually prepared to make sudden decisions and would therefore be best suited to a managerial position. The best days of the week for you are Monday and Thursday; your lucky numbers are 1 and 6. The colours best suited to your temperament are orange and bluish white.

You are a person who is interested in material wealth. You have strong beliefs and opinions and you appreciate privacy. You would be best suited to a career in the jewellery industry or an executive position in the world of finance. The lucky days of the week for you are Mondays and Wednesdays. The colours best suited to you are grey, green or black.

This card signifies that you have a warm and friendly nature and that you are very proud of your home and family. In the employment field you are best suited to the real estate industry or the building trade. Best days of the week for you are Tuesday and Friday. Your lucky numbers are 2 and 3 and your colours are white and yellow.

This card suggests that you are a person with a jealous and possessive nature. You would probably be best suited to a position in a government department. The best days of the week are Thursday and Sunday; your lucky numbers are 4 and 8. The best colours for you to be associated with are blue and maroon.

This card indicates that you are broad-minded and have a good general knowledge. You are probably the type of person who is willing to try anything once. You like to travel and are therefore best suited to jobs in the travel industry. Best days of the week are Saturday and Thursday; lucky numbers are 7 and 8; colours are pale brown and white.

This card reflects that you are a person who is mainly interested in the luxuries that life can offer. You are also interested in the economy and in home life in general. You are therefore best suited to being an accountant or solicitor or to any job within the finance industry. Lucky numbers are 2 and 7; good days of the week are Monday and Saturday; colours are white, black or green.

You are a humanitarian and have an open mind towards other people's beliefs. You would therefore be best suited to a job in the ministry or as a social worker. Lucky numbers are 3 and 9; good days of the week are Sunday and Wednesday; colours are pale pink or strawberry.

You are broad-minded and have a deep concern for others. You are intellectually oriented and would be best suited to a job in the medical field. Lucky numbers are 1 and 5; best days of the week are Sunday and Thursday; colours are pink and blue.

Selection of this card indicates a person who will be fairly successful throughout life and one who can cope with most situations. You are creative and inventive and would be best suited to a technical trade or profession. Lucky numbers are 6 and 9; colours are orange and white; days are Friday and Tuesday.

9 ♦

You are the life of the party and full of surprises! People like you are suited to any job and are the proverbial "Jack of all trades". No numbers are unlucky for you and almost all colours suit you. There is no such thing as an unlucky day for you.

9 ♥

You are likely to be a daydreamer and you plan and wish for many things; however, some of your wishes do come true. You are best suited to a clerical or secretarial job. Colours are white, black and grey; numbers are 2 and 9; days of the week are Monday and Friday.

9 ♠

This card signifies that you will suffer many delays and disappointments throughout life. You might possibly have heart or chest problems, so you should try and lead a healthy lifestyle. You are best suited to housekeeping or labouring jobs although a lot of office workers tend to draw this card. Lucky numbers are 9 and 18; colours are blue and maroon; best days of the week are Wednesday and Thursday.

8 ♣

You are a very good communicator and are best suited to the job of disc jockey, telephone operator, or a position that brings you into contact with the public. The best days of the week are Thursday and Sunday; best colours are pink, strawberry and red. Lucky numbers are 5 and 8.

8 ♦

You are fairly moody and given to frequent changes of mood. This card usually indicates a person who is self-employed. Lucky numbers are 8 and 9; colours are dark brown and purple; best day of the week is Friday.

8 ♥

You are a person who tries hard in all aspects of life. Some people don't work hard at maintaining relationships, but you are best suited to doing this. Best days of the week are Sunday and Monday; colours are green and grey. Lucky numbers are 1 and 8.

8 ♠

People are attracted to you and you probably have a large circle of friends. You are quite possibly a lawyer or involved in the legal profession. Best days of the week are Monday and Tuesday; colours are blue and red; lucky numbers are 1 and 3.

7 ♣

This card reveals one who is very family orientated and likes clubs and large groups of people. You are best suited to work in a library, family planning clinic, or any work which involves organising people and their interests. Colours are blue, green and maroon; lucky numbers are 4 and 7; best days of the week are Saturday and Wednesday.

7 ♦

This card represents a bookworm and a person who can cope with the stress and strain of life. You would be well suited to work in politics or as a university lecturer or any job that involves paperwork (and lots of it). Best days of the week are Saturday and Tuesday; colours are yellow and white; lucky numbers are 8 and 9.

7 ♥

This card represents one who has a great deal of artistic ability and an interest in clairvoyance. You would do well in the art industry. Lucky numbers are 7 and 9; best days of the week are Saturday and Monday. For you there is no such thing as an unlucky colour.

7 ♠

This card reflects one who is prone to ailments such as asthma and sinusitis. You are an affectionate person and need a job that brings you into contact with people. Lucky numbers are 4 and 8; best days of the week are Saturday and Tuesday; colours are black and green.

You are very close to those whom you love and in order to be happy you need the security of a family. You would do well working in a hospital or child care centre. Lucky numbers are 3 and 6; colours are black and blue; best days of the week are Tuesday and Friday.

You are an independent person and would like to own and operate your own business in the future. You would enjoy work as a salesperson. Lucky numbers are 5 and 7; colours are pale brown or red; best days of the week are Saturday and Thursday.

You are likely to suffer from anxiety and nervous trouble. Although a position of authority is not recommended, you might. find yourself working as a manager of a large firm, or in work connected with taxation. You will probably marry late in life. Lucky numbers are 1 and 6; colours are grey and dark brown; best days of the week are Saturday and Sunday.

You are probably uncertain and nervous, and more than likely bite your fingernails. You are likely to work in the prison service or similar jobs that are liable to cause stress. Lucky numbers are 6 and 8; colours are yellow and orange; best days of the week are Thursday and Saturday.

You have deep thoughts on many subjects and possibly like to philosophise. You will gain much success through study and concentration and are suited to a career in science. Lucky numbers are 2 and 5; best days of the week are Tuesday and Friday; colours are white and pink.

5♦

You enjoy study, mainly on business subjects, and are more than likely a successful business person. Colours are orange and pink; lucky numbers are 3 and 6; best days of the week are Tuesday and Wednesday.

5♥

You are flirtatious and because of this are destined to have trouble with relationships. Your work probably entails a good deal of travel. Colours are pale brown and red; lucky numbers are 5 and 7; best days of the week are Thursday and Saturday.

5♠

Little things will cause you to become anxious. You probably find it hard to communicate with other people and difficult to get a job, and when you do, you fear you will lose it. Try to assert yourself and become more confident. Lucky numbers are 5 and 9; colours are deep red and dark brown; best days are Thursday and Sunday.

4♣

You are a hard worker, particularly with manual jobs, and are therefore suited to working in the building and construction industry or to being a council worker. Lucky numbers are 1 and 4; colours are grey and blue; best days of the week are Sunday and Wednesday.

4♦

You are a person who is lucky in lotteries and games of chance. Luck seems to be attracted to you. Any number you choose will normally bring you luck. Best days of the week are Monday and Friday; colours are orange and white.

4♥

People who like uniforms usually draw this card. You are probably intellectual and are best suited to a job in the armed forces or any other field of work that requires you to wear a uniform. Best days of the week are Thursday and Friday; lucky numbers are 5 and 6; colours are pink and green.

4♠

You tend to have a negative approach to everything. You are not very lucky and will quite likely be married more than once. You also need to take good care of your health. The days of the week when you feel slightly optimistic are Wednesday and Thursday. You probably find it very hard to work in any field of employment successfully. Not many colours brighten you but black and grey suit you best. Although few numbers are attracted to you, 4, 6 and 8 might possibly bring you luck.

3♣

You characteristically go out of your way to help others, particularly family and friends. You are best suited to teaching. Best days of the week are Wednesday and Friday; lucky numbers are 6 and 9; colours are light brown or cream.

3♦

You are a nature lover and a possible health fanatic. You will work best in a small corporation run by your own family. Lucky numbers are 4 and 7; best days of the week are Monday and Friday; colours are maroon and blue.

3♥

You are an intellectual and you do not mind sharing your knowledge; therefore you are best suited to teaching older children. Lucky numbers are 3 and 5; colours are strawberry and pink; best days of the week are Wednesday and Saturday.

3♠

You are a worrier and you tend to overprotect your loved ones. You are best suited to a hotel or restaurant environment. Lucky numbers are 3 and 7; best days of the week are Tuesday and Friday; colours are red and brown.

2♣

You are a person who enjoys having a good time, possibly in the night spots. You are best suited to shift work. Colours are yellow and pink; best days of the week are Friday and Saturday; lucky numbers are 2 and 8.

2 ♦

You are a person who appreciates the company of good friends and would therefore make an excellent business partner. Lucky days are Wednesday and Friday; lucky numbers are 2 and 3; colours are blue and yellow.

2 ♥

You are a very affectionate and loving person. The kind of work that best suits you is as a medical practitioner, nurse, airline steward or stewardess. Lucky numbers are 2 and 4; best days are Monday and Thursday; colours are pink and blue.

2 ♠

This card represents a divorced person or one who has trouble handling relationships. You are best suited to running a small business or being a veterinarian, psychologist or psychiatrist . Colours are orange and green; best days of the week are Saturday and Sunday; lucky numbers are 4 and 6.

This is an entertaining party game in which the 12 court cards are divided into two groups — one group is for the males and contains the four Queens and the other is for the females and contains the four Kings and four Jacks. The two separate packs are held face down by one member of the party (the dealer), while the males select a Queen and the females select a King or Jack as their "perfect partner". Once everyone has selected a partner the dealer must select from the pack a partner that suits him or her. Only 12 people at a time can play this game, unless extra court cards are used from other packs.

The key to your perfect partner is in the following pages.

A man over the age of 25, more dark than fair, with brown eyes and of a very caring nature. Possibly an artist, musician, or businessman.

A man over the age of 25 with blue, grey or green eyes and very fair or red hair. An intellectual person, possibly a government worker or a uniformed man.

A man over the age of 25 with hazel or green eyes and whose hair is more fair than dark. A charming person, possibly a salesman.

A man over the age of 25 with very dark eyes, dark hair and a dark complexion. One who has an earthy quality and who loves nature.

A woman more dark than fair with brown eyes, of a pleasing personality, possibly a nurse, doctor or teacher.

A woman with blue, green or grey eyes and very fair, blonde, red or grey hair. One who is potentially a good businesswoman.

A woman more fair than dark, with hazel or green eyes, possibly of a jealous nature. One who would be suited to a secretarial or executive position.

A woman with dark eyes, very dark hair and a dark complexion. One who has a motherly disposition and who would be a good home-maker.

A man up to the age of 25, more dark than fair, with brown eyes and of a pleasant disposition. He will make an excellent father, and could quite possibly be a young businessman.

A man up to the age of 25 with blue, grey or green eyes and very fair or red hair. An intellectual, he could possibly be a banker or a accountant.

A man up to the age of 25 with hazel or green eyes and whose hair is more fair than dark. A person with a caring personality, he could possibly be a solicitor, lawyer, or doctor.

A man up to the age of 25 with very dark eyes, dark hair and a dark complexion. He could be a person who works in the building and construction industry.

PART III
CASE HISTORIES

CARD READINGS

To become proficient at cartomancy, or indeed at any other art, it is necessary to monitor your own progress — to see where you have been right or wrong and to make amends accordingly. In doing readings for another person it is very hard to check whether your predictions have been accurate or not. As a consequence, one of the most valuable experiences you can have as a cartomancer is for a client to come back and tell you how the predictions turned out.

In this regard, I am sincerely grateful for having had clients return for subsequent readings and for allowing me to describe in this book the earlier readings I gave them and the actual events that occurred.

The case histories presented in this section differ from the previous example readings in that some of the predictions did not come from the meanings of the cards alone. Rather, they were obtained through a combination of cartomancy and my natural psychic abilities, which I have developed during my thirteen years of reading. I believe that everyone has natural psychic abilities, which can be developed to quite high levels.

Usually the cards give you only the basic outlines of future events. With the aid of natural psychic abilities, however, you can clarify events or at least add more information to the prediction. The following case histories show how the use of natural psychic abilities combined with the art of cartomancy has enhanced my readings. Once you have reached this level of self-development you can expect an equivalent degree of fluency and accuracy in your own readings.

One thing that any clairvoyant or reader should always keep in mind is the enquirer's feelings. Many people seek the guidance of a clairvoyant when they are troubled or worried about a particular problem. Whenever a person seeks my guidance I try to the best of my ability to give them secure, sound guidance. I do not believe in hiding anything from any of my clients, but with psychic ability comes the responsibility not to frighten or offend with rash statements, especially if they concern misfortunes on a personal level (such as deaths, accidents or the like). If these circumstances should arise, it is the responsibility of the reader to present them in a caring way, so as to prepare the enquirer and help him or her cope with any misfortunes when they occur.

VERNA

When Verna came to see me for a reading, she needed guidance in several areas of her life. I decided to use Della's method for the reading, and as Verna is 40 and has red hair, I chose the Queen of Diamonds to signify her.

The immediate influence was the Ace of Hearts, reversed; the 4 of Hearts, reversed; and the Queen of Hearts. From these cards I concluded that Verna would soon be having difficulties with another female at her home, possibly her daughter, which could result in her daughter leaving within a period of four weeks or months.

The remaining cards fell in the following order:

Ace of Spades 3 of Hearts, reversed 8 of Spades 6 of Hearts	Within a period of six months, Verna would be meeting a new aquaintance who would be having some legal dealings in a government building.
Queen of Diamonds Ace of Hearts 8 of Diamonds 9 of Spades	Within a period of 9, Verna would be changing her address, and amidst all of this she would experience delays and disappointments.
Queen of Clubs 9 of Clubs, reversed King of Hearts 2 of Hearts	I felt the Queen of Clubs to be another of Verna's daughters, who would be enjoying success in her career though a promotion or new line of work, as well as a happy relationship.

8 of Hearts *Ace of Clubs* *10 of Spades,* *reversed* *8 of Clubs*	In a period of 8, Verna would take on a new job, but it would be for only a short time.
Jack of Hearts *Jack of Clubs* *4 of Hearts,* *reversed* *7 of Spades*	Within a period of 7, there would be news of two young boys playing together, one of whom would be injured slightly.
9 of Diamonds *King of Clubs* *10 of Hearts* *7 of Hearts*	Verna would be receiving a surprise gift, possibly of flowers, from a male with brown hair in a period of 7.
9 of Hearts *10 of Clubs* *Queen of Spades* *10 of Diamonds*	I read this to mean that Verna wished to travel overseas, and also that she would either have property dealings or would be sharing some land with a dark-haired female in a period of 10.
Queen of Hearts *7 of Clubs* *King of Spades* *Ace of Diamonds*	Within a period of 7, wedding arrangements would be made, involving a dark-haired middle-aged male.
King of Diamonds *Jack of Spades* *Jack of Diamonds* *7 of Diamonds*	Verna would be meeting a group of three males for financial discussions, all of which would turn out in her favour.

Three months after this reading Verna returned to me for a second reading, and she informed me that my first reading had been quite accurate. Her young daughter had left home. Some of Verna's friends were having legal difficulties, she was changing address, and she had taken on a job that did not suit her and so had resigned. Her eldest daughter was involved in a new romance, and had been successful in her career. Also, an ex-boyfriend had sent Verna a bunch of flowers, and a young friend of hers had hurt himself. However, she was still waiting for her marriage, overseas trip, and property and financial dealings.

CASE HISTORIES

ANDREW

ANDREW

When Andrew came to me for a consultation his main concerns were his social life and several business deals that he was negotiating. For his reading I chose the Romany Method. Andrew is 44 and has fair hair, so I signified him as the King of Diamonds.

The immediate influence was the King of Clubs, the 10 of Diamonds, and the King of Hearts. This indicated that Andrew would quite soon be spending a large amount of money on his own business.

The remaining cards fell in the following order:

Ace of Hearts Ace of Clubs 8 of Spades, reversed 10 of Hearts 3 of Hearts	In a period of 3, Andrew would be meeting some old friends, who had some connection with Melbourne.
King of Diamonds King of Spades 9 of Diamonds, reversed 9 of Clubs 6 of Hearts, reversed	Andrew would be going into business with a male over the age of 25 and with an olive complexion. I felt that the business, which would involve borrowing money, was either electronically or mechanically based and that there would be a lot of anxiety associated with it, but that in a period of six months it would all be sorted out.
10 of Clubs 10 of Spades King of Hearts 7 of Diamonds 4 of Hearts	There would soon be news from overseas regarding a male over 25, who would require hospitalisation, although not for a serious problem, and he would recover satisfactorily.
Queen of Spades 2 of Hearts Ace of Diamonds 9 of Spades 7 of Hearts	Marriage was indicated with a female of dark hair and dark eyes, possibly with a name starting with "R", but there would be a number of disappointments before everything went ahead fully. New ideas would help to solve these problems, but the final resolution would occur within a period of 7.

Jack of Hearts, reversed *Ace of Spades* *8 of Hearts, reversed* *9 of Hearts*	I concluded that Andrew would be having some official dealings, perhaps with a solicitor, which would require an important decision and would work out in his favour.
Jack of Clubs *Jack of Diamonds, reversed* *8 of Diamonds* *8 of Clubs*	There would be discussions with an accountant, who might have dark hair, within a period of 8.
7 of Spades *Queen of Diamonds* *Queen of Hearts* *Jack of Spades, reversed*	A female friend of Andrew's was likely to have considerable difficulties dealing with a young bachelor.
10 of Diamonds *King of Clubs* *Queen of Clubs* *7 of Clubs*	Andrew would have some business dealings, probably with a wealthy female, in a period of seven months.

Six months later Andrew returned to my home for another reading. He informed me that he had found the woman of his dreams, and that after a few hassles, his business life was beginning to correct itself. Also, he had travelled to Melbourne four weeks after the reading and met up with some old friends. His business appeared to be taking an electronics slant, and he had recently received news of a friend overseas who had gone into hospital. He was still waiting for the wealthy female to turn up for his business.

TONY

Tony came to me simply out of curiousity to see what lay in store for him. Having never had a reading before, he was quite happy to allow me to do it by whatever means I wished — I chose Della's Method. I signified him as the Jack of Hearts, because he was 24 and had fair hair and blue eyes.

The immediate influence was the 10 of Clubs, the 3 of Hearts and the 10 of Diamonds. From this I concluded that within a period of three months Tony would be spending a large sum of money to travel overseas.

The remaining cards were:

10 of Diamonds 6 of Hearts Ace of Spades 4 of Hearts	A large amount of money would be coming to Tony from the defence forces, probably the Navy. However, I felt that there would be some anxiety connected with this before it eventuated.
10 of Clubs 7 of Spades 3 of Hearts 8 of Diamonds	Tony would be travelling overseas within a period of three months. His plans might change because of a few minor disappointments.
Queen of Spades 10 of Hearts 2 of Hearts 8 of Clubs	I felt that Tony would be having a relationship with a dark-haired female from overseas, within a period of 8.
King of Hearts 10 of Spades 7 of Diamonds 7 of Clubs	There would be news of Tony's father going into hospital, and he would recover within a period of 7.

7 of Hearts,
   reversed
Ace of Clubs,
   reversed
9 of Spades
8 of Spades
	This indicated to me that Tony possessed quite strong psychic abilities of his own, and that he would always be forewarned of impending disasters.

Queen of Diamonds Queen of Clubs, reversed 9 of Diamonds 9 of Clubs	A fair-haired woman, probably his sister, would need treatment for a minor medical condition within a period of 9.
Ace of Hearts Jack of Hearts Jack of Diamonds 8 of Hearts	This indicated that a change of residence was likely in the near future, and that he might be sharing a house with two other young men.
King of Diamonds	Tony's health would always be good, and

9 of Hearts	he would meet two young males, both
Jack of Spades	darker than himself, who would develop
Jack of Clubs	into lifelong friends.

King of Clubs	There would be news of a wedding
Ace of Diamonds	between a dark-haired male and a
Queen of Hearts	brown-haired female who might have
King of Spades	some business connections.

Two months later, Tony contacted me again. During our conversation he told me that several of my predictions had already come to pass. He was planning to go overseas once his termination payment came through from the Navy. He had been psychically warned once; specifically, about the gas leak on board the HMAS *Stalwart*. He had changed his address, and his sister had gone into hospital to have a baby. So far, his father had not been hospitalised, but Tony did meet his dark-haired female and had just been given a wedding invitation.

JEFF

Jeff came to see me because he was concerned about the business he was trying to establish. He felt that he needed some guidance and hoped that I would be able to help him. Again, I used Della's Method for the reading. Jeff has an olive complexion and dark hair and is 36 years old — he was therefore signified by the King of Spades.

The immediate influence was the 8 of Hearts; the 8 of Diamonds and the Queen of Spades, which suggested an unexpected relationship with a female who had dark hair and brown eyes, within a period of 8.

The remaining cards fell in the following order:

8 of Hearts	This indicated that Jeff would be having
3 of Hearts	business dealings to do with an office
King of Spades	building in a period of four months.
King of Diamonds	
4 of Hearts	

10 of Clubs	Jeff was going through a major change in
8 of Diamonds	residence, possibly involving travel to

Ace of Hearts *7 of Spades* *2 of Hearts*	another country, which would be completed within a period of 2.
Ace of Clubs *King of Clubs* *9 of Diamonds* *8 of Clubs* *7 of Hearts*	There would soon be unexpected contact with a friend in Brisbane, within a period of 7.
Ace of Diamonds *10 of Hearts* *7 of Clubs,* *reversed* *9 of Clubs* *Queen of Hearts*	Jeff would have contact with a church and a large group of people, but not for a wedding or funeral.
Queen of Clubs *7 of Diamonds* *Jack of Clubs* *Jack of Spades*	This indicated to me that Jeff would be having business dealings with a dark-haired female within a period of seven months.
Jack of Hearts *6 of Hearts* *9 of Spades* *10 of Spades*	Jeff would soon be in contact with a close friend whose name I felt would begin with the letter "J"; this friend would be going through a lot of major disappointments.
Queen of Diamonds *Queen of Spades* *8 of Spades,* *reversed* *10 of Diamonds*	A close female friend with fair hair would visit or contact him from overseas within a period of ten weeks.
Ace of Spades *King of Hearts* *Jack of Diamonds,* *reversed* *9 of Hearts*	Jeff would be contacted within a period of 9 by a government employee working in Brisbane.

Jeff saw me one month later and reported, to my surprise, that not one single prediction had eventuated. We then met a further four months later, and I discovered that the majority of the reading had been correct. He was planning to establish his own business and had been trying to obtain a small office to work from. He had finalised his immigration from New Zealand, had been contacted by friends from Brisbane, and had started studying Chinese at a Presbyterian church. A close female friend whom Jeff used to work with in New Zealand had come to visit him, and he had received a letter from his friend John, who was having severe personal problems. The only predictions still to be fulfilled were the business dealings with a female and contact with a government employee in Brisbane.

KAREN

When Karen came to see me she was deeply concerned over her current relationship. I informed her that the playing cards would provide good advice, because they would indicate events affecting not only her but also other people around her. I used the "destiny in 52 cards" method of reading. Karen is 28 and more fair than dark, so I signified her by the Queen of Hearts.

The immediate influence was the King of Clubs, the Queen of Spades, and the 5 of Hearts. It was apparent that Karen was having a troubled relationship with a male over the age of 25 with dark hair, who I felt was seeing another woman.

The pathfinder was the signifier (the Queen of Hearts), the 3 of Hearts, the Ace of Clubs, and the 2 of Clubs. I advised Karen that she needed a break and that perhaps she should consider taking a trip to see some supportive friends or relatives. (At this point, Karen told me that she was contemplating doing just that.)

The cards fell in the following order:

9 of Clubs	Karen would be taking on a new line of
7 of Hearts	work, and would probably have a female
Queen of Clubs	boss. This was going to occur within a
5 of Diamonds	period of five weeks to five months.
10 of Clubs	An elderly male from Queensland would
7 of Clubs	visit her but his plans would be delayed
9 of Spades	and he would not arrive as scheduled.
King of Diamonds	
8 of Hearts	Karen's new work would provide her
8 of Diamonds	with the opportunity to socialise more,

Queen of Diamonds 10 of Hearts	and she would probably have the company of a fair-haired female.
Ace of Hearts 3 of Clubs Jack of Hearts 4 of Diamonds	A change around the home was likely for Karen, and in a period of 4 she would be receiving practical assistance from a young brown-haired male.
2 of Diamonds Queen of Spades 7 of Diamonds 6 of Clubs	There would be news of a dark-haired female friend entering into a business partnership in a period of six months.
5 of Clubs King of Clubs 2 of Hearts 4 of Spades	There would be a fresh start in Karen's relationship, but there would still be a number of significant problems to be sorted out.
6 of Diamonds 3 of Spades Jack of Clubs 4 of Clubs	Karen would receive news of a young dark-haired male having a lot of concerns to work through in his personal life.
King of Hearts 10 of Diamonds 8 of Clubs 5 of Hearts	Karen would be discussing her personal problems with a brown-haired middle-aged male who was financially secure and lived in the country.
10 of Spades Jack of Diamonds 6 of Hearts 2 of Spades	There would be news of a young fair-haired male requiring hospital treatment within a period of two months.
9 of Diamonds King of Spades 8 of Spades 6 of Spades	Financial assistance would come to Karen through a dark-haired male, thus removing much of the anxiety around her.
Ace of Spades 4 of Hearts 3 of Diamonds Jack of Spades	Karen would be having contact within a period of four weeks with a young brown-haired male who worked for the government.
Ace of Diamonds 9 of Hearts 7 of Spades	Karen's wish was to have the problems in her relationship solved so that she could eventually get married. However, I felt

5 of Spades   that this was a long way off, if ever, and I could
see her married to another man.

Three months later Karen contacted me to discuss the predictions
I had made for her. She informed me that her father had planned
to travel from Queensland to visit her, but his trip had had to be
postponed; and that she had taken a new job, which was giving
her a lot of inner satisfaction, as she was beginning to socialise to
a greater extent. Also, she was changing the decor of her flat. The
older male that had been mentioned in the reading was a very
dear friend from the country, who was helping her to come to
terms with her personal problems. Her boyfriend had come back
to her, but she was still having trouble with the relationship. She
was still waiting for the other predictions to eventuate, especially
meeting the new man that she was eventually to marry.

CONCLUSION

By writing this book I hope I have been able to show people interested in the art of cartomancy the easy and varied ways in which this knowledge can be applied.

Once the student has been able to master the methods described in this book, he or she should then be able to learn to read the ancient Tarot pack, which, as previously mentioned, is the ancestor of the playing cards.

My aim in writing this book has been both to teach the student and to show others that cartomancy can be used not only to predict the future but also the light-hearted way in which cards can be used for party games.

The example readings used in this book were based on actual readings done for family and friends. Since the completion of the book 85 per cent of the predictions have eventuated. By this you will see that it is possible to attain a fair degree of accuracy once you have mastered the ancient art of fortune-telling by the cards.

GLOSSARY

arcanas (major and minor)	The two packs belonging to the Tarot pack.
cartomancer	One who uses cards for the art of fortune-telling.
cartomancy	The practice of fortune-telling by cards.
court cards	The 12 cards of the pack used to describe people.
enquirer	The one seeking to have his or her fortune told by the cards.
immediate influence	The three cards that are revealed once each pile of cards has been inverted.
lay, the	The four cards laid out at a time.
period of	Time in which a certain event will take place.
pathfinder	Another phrase for the immediate influence.
reader	The clairvoyant.
reversed	Inverted position (upside down).
signifier	The court card used to signify the enquirer.
Tarot pack	The first pack of cards developed to divine the future.